Beginner's Guide to PAINTING ON WOOD

By Betty Padden

CONTENTS

WOODCARVING ILLUSTRATED

Introduction

Whether you are a beginner or an advanced carver, it is imperative to learn how to paint. As we all know, a poor paint job leaves much to be desired—even on the best carves.

This booklet walks you through four seasonal projects utilizing four painting styles. I've included patterns in the back if you'd like to carve your own plaques, although the painting techniques described can be applied to any carve. You will learn about blending, highlights, shadows, and more. As you read along, you'll discover the painting process is nothing to fear. With a little patience and practice, you may even enjoy it as much as carving. For each article, one "pea" refers to a pea-sized drop of paint.

Useful Tips

Planning Ahead

Create your color scheme before you start painting. For example, I decided I wanted to paint the tulips (Painting With Acrylics, page 5) purple with green leaves. I wanted the flowers to pop off the background, so I chose a neutral taupe background to create a good contrast. Color matching can be a challenge. Check paint stores and online for resources to guide you in pairing colors.

Mixing Colors

When mixing colors, always add small amounts of a darker color to a lighter one. A little bit of a dark color goes a long way; however, if you add a light color to a dark color, you will have to mix a lot of paint to achieve your desired shade.

How To Blend Colors

Blending is one of the biggest stress points for most beginning painters, but it is essential to producing a good painting. This simple technique makes the difference between an amateurish paint job and an admirable one.

We will be using wet-to-wet techniques (methods that blend paint right on the piece while it is still wet) for blending colors on a carved piece. One technique requires you to sweep the brush back and forth to blend two colors (pictured below). An easier technique is stippling, which involves firmly tapping the border between two colors until they blend together (pictured at bottom).

Techniques for blending: Sweeping, at right; Stippling, shown below.

Paintbrush Care

Learn to select, clean, and store your brushes like a pro

Selecting paintbrushes can be a daunting task given the array of choices, but knowing the basics can make a world of difference! I'm here to break down the different types, shapes and sizes, and their uses. I'll also cover brush cleaning and storage. As you use them, your brushes will become like old friends—much like your chisels and gouges; you'll start to know how they will perform in a given situation. Care for these tools correctly and you'll be able to use them for years!

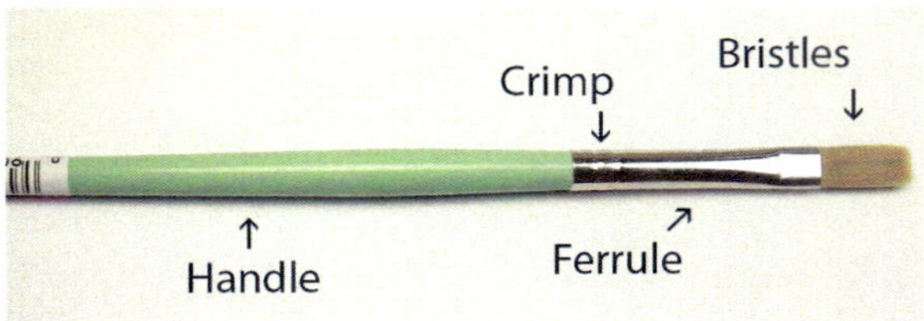

Bristles

Naturally, the bristles are the most important part of the brush. They are made either with synthetic fibers (these are very "springy" and smooth in texture), natural fibers (hair of various animals—kolinsky sable, pony, hog, etc.) or a combination of the two fibers.

Natural bristles have barbs or scales, which make them thicker, stiffer, and a little harder to clean. Due to their stiffness, natural bristle brushes are mainly used for canvas painting with thicker paint. Typically, they are more expensive than synthetic brushes; however, some can be less expensive than the synthetic options.

Synthetic brushes, which are smoother and springier than their natural counterparts, go with a variety of paints and are typically easier to clean. I use mainly synthetic brushes for applying paint, but I reserve some natural bristle brushes for blending. Pricing depends on the size; I spend $3-$5 on smaller brushes and $10-$15 on larger ones. However, buying a set is usually cheaper.

Bristle Shapes

Rounds
Workhorse of the set; used for applying paint and washes.

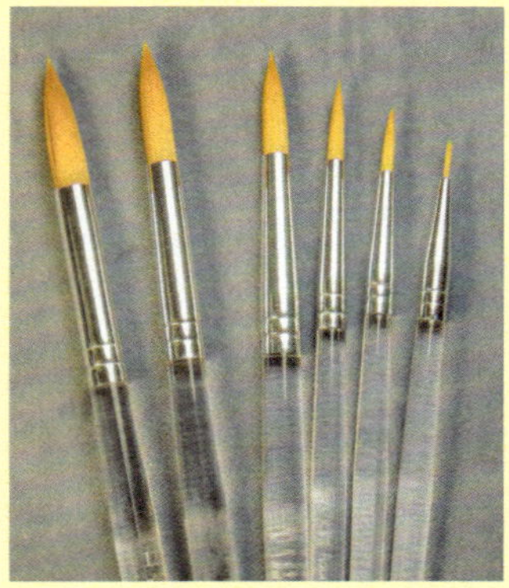

Flats
Used for painting large areas and adding textures, such as house or roof details.

Angled flats
Used like regular flats, but tip can reach into smaller areas.

Filberts
Good for blending or painting a soft edge.

Bristle Shapes

Script liners
Used for fine lines and details.

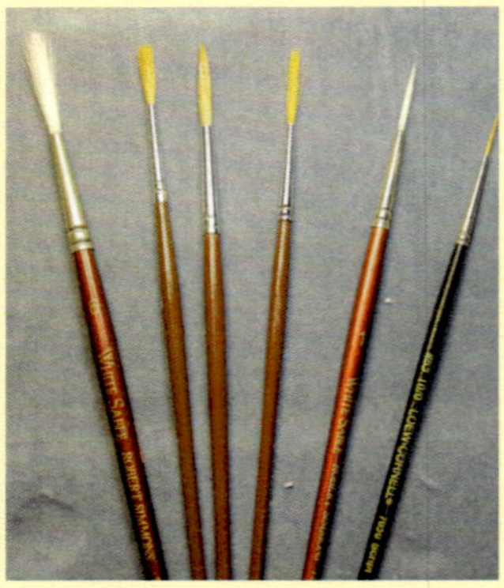

Blenders
Used to blur the border between two colors to form a gradation of color.

Fan brushes
Used to paint textured areas like clouds, trees, or leaves.

"Spoiled" brushes
Great for blending and adding texture (It may be the Yankee in me, but I have a hard time throwing a brush out!).

Washing Your Brushes

When using acrylics, have a container of water ready to wash your brushes instantly because the paint dries so quickly. *Note: It is safe to wash acrylic paint off in your work or household sink. Use warm—not hot—water; hot water can cause the glue used to secure the bristles to fail.*

Clean your oil paint brushes in a paint thinner before washing with water. *Note: You can leave your paint thinner in a sealed jar, let the pigment settle, and reuse at a later time. Be sure to collect oil paint sludge and dispose of it at your local hazardous waste site.* Do your best to remove all the paint, especially from the ferrule; paint left to dry here will cause the bristles to splay out and separate.

After you wash your brushes in paint thinner and squeeze them with a cloth, give them a final wash with a brush cleaner; I like The Master's Brush Cleaner (use as directed). A good brush cleaner will even restore a brush with hardened paint on it to some degree. Shape the bristles while they are wet and let them air dry.

Storing Your Brushes

Store your brushes upright in a container so the bristles don't bend. I use a simple jar for organized storage and easy access. You can get carriers of all sizes at any art supply store if you need to transport your brushes and other painting supplies.

Painting with Acrylics

Learn to add highlights and shadows in this springtime design

For the Spring Tulips, we will be using acrylic paints over a primed carving. I like Jo Sonja acrylics, which dry flat, have a creamy consistency with good pigmentation, while remaining affordable.

Acrylics have some pros and cons. They dry fast, so you can repaint quickly. They are readily available, they are easy to clean up with water, and you can add shadows or subtle highlights even after the paint is dry. The fast-drying nature of the paints does require you to work quickly to use the wet blending techniques I describe. Acrylic paint colors can darken as they dry, and you need to apply a sealer for exterior use. Acrylic paint colors are also not as rich as oil paint colors.

Getting Started

Set up a paint palette. I mix paints on aluminum foil because it's waterproof and can keep paint workable for a day or two when properly sealed. *Note: To seal, collect the paint in a pile and fold the foil over the paint. Press out as much air as possible, and then fold over the edges.*

PREPARING THE CARVING

1 **Prime the entire carving.** Apply two coats of a good exterior latex primer to the front and back of the carving. Be sure the final strokes of the brush go in a uniform horizontal direction.

PAINTING THE DETAILS

2 **Basecoat the background.** Mix 1 pea yellow ochre with 1½ pea burnt umber and 18 pea white (this color will be the highlights when you add the darker colors in the final coat). Paint the background and sides of the frame, leaves, and flowers using the biggest brush you feel comfortable with. Keep the final strokes going in the same direction. If the paint on the palette starts to dry, mix in a little water to freshen it. Seal the paint in the palette for later use.

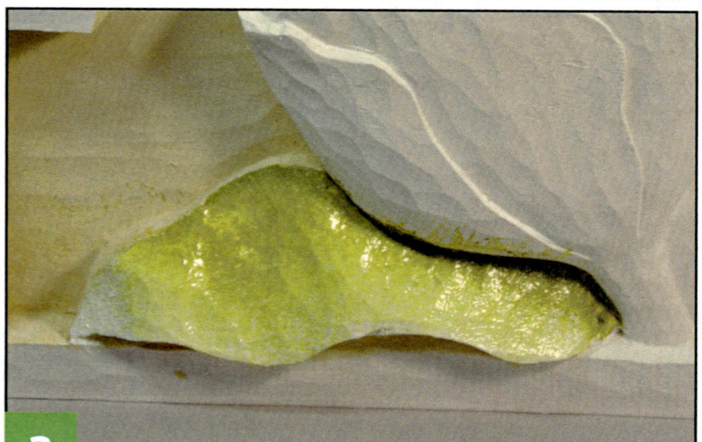

3 **Basecoat the leaves.** Mix ¼ pea sap green, ¼ pea black, and 12 peas yellow to make a light green. Paint white on the upper edges and tip of leaf 1 and green on the rest. Firmly tap (stipple) the border between the two colors until they blend together and you can no longer see where one color begins and the other ends. Repeat for all of the leaves and stems in the order they were carved. Use a generous amount of paint, and continue stippling the paint until it is well blended.

4 **Basecoat the tulips.** Mix ¼ pea Payne's gray with ¼ pea burgundy and 12 peas white. Apply this light purple to a petal. Load one side of a blending brush with white, and rotate the brush so the white paint will hit the edges of the petal. Stipple the paint until the two colors are well blended. Repeat the process with the other petals in the order they were carved.

5 **Add the darker green.** Mix 1 pea sap green, 1 pea black, and 2 peas yellow. On leaf 1, apply the basecoat mix (saved from Step 3) to the outer edges. Paint the darker green in the center and stipple to blend the two. Load a clean, dry blending brush with white and stipple highlights on the tips of the leaves. Repeat on the other leaves, adding some highlights to the upper edges of leaf 3. Paint the stems light green and highlight them by stippling white on one side.

6 **Paint the leaf veins.** Mix white into the light green to make a light celery color. Using a script liner brush, add a little water to the paint to make it creamy but not runny. Load the brush by scrubbing it into the paint to flatten and load it. Flip it over and do the same to the other side of the brush. Notice the flat, chisel-like edge it now has. Use the thin edge to paint the veins.

7 **Add the middle tone of purple.** Mix 1 pea Payne's gray with 1 pea burgundy and 2 peas white. Apply this to the lower third of the petals, and then tap some white on the edges of the petals. Use a clean, damp brush to sweep the purple to the edge. Clean and dry the brush, and then sweep the white down. Repeat for all of the petals. Notice how the brush strokes enhance the curve of the petals.

8 **Add the darkest purple.** Mix 1 pea Payne's gray with 1 pea burgundy. Use a clean, damp brush to sweep this color up to the edges of the petals, leaving the raised ripples lighter and thoroughly blending the purple (see Step 10 photo below).

9 **Paint the frame.** Mix 1 pea yellow ochre, 1 pea burnt umber, and 1 pea white. Paint the raised frame, the outside edges, and the back of the carving.

materials & **tools**

MATERIALS

- Pine, 1¾" (4.4cm) thick: 8¾" x 14" (22.2cm x 35.6cm)
- Exterior latex primer
- Acrylic paints, such as Jo Sonja: burgundy, burnt umber, lamp black, light yellow, Payne's gray, sap green, titanium white, yellow ochre
- Container for water
- Paint rag or paper towels
- Sandpaper
- Aluminum foil

The author used these products for the project. Substitute your choice of brands, tools, and materials as desired.

TOOLS

- Assort paintbrushes: round, flats synthetic, bristle blenders
- #1 script liner

Using Oil Paints

Harness the rich tones of oil paint in one summery plaque

This project shows you how to paint oils on a basswood carving without using a primer. Projects carved from basswood and painted with oils will not withstand the weather well, so I recommend keeping it indoors.

Decide on a color scheme before you begin. I will use a summer sky as a background for the yellow sunflower with its brown center and a queen butterfly. The queen butterfly is similar to a monarch, except the wing background color is a darker, rusty reddish-orange rather than the bright orange of a monarch.

Painting with Oils on Raw Wood

There are many benefits to painting with oils on raw (unprimed) wood. For example, the long drying time of these paints means that even a beginner can blend them without difficulty, and they do not darken as they dry like acrylic and latex paints do. In addition, oil paints dry to a matte finish, which means you can easily add darker shadows even after the paint is dry.

Most people object to the long drying time and smelly thinners and cleaners used with oil paints. However, oils dry faster on raw wood and you can mix solutions with the paints to speed up the drying time. Odorless thinners are available, as well.

Getting Started

Use the pattern on page 22 and your choice of tools to carve the piece. Once you have finished the carving, you can start painting immediately—no other preparation is needed.

- Thin all of the paints slightly with paint thinner (not water), unless otherwise stated.
- I use pea-size amounts of paint because that amount, when mixed with other colors and thinned slightly, is usually enough for the project without a lot of waste. You'll see that I give paint measurements in peas, or ¼" (6mm) globs.

PAINTING THE BACKGROUND & LEAVES

1 **Paint the background sky.** Mix ½ pea raw sienna with 6 peas Prussian blue, 1 pea Payne's gray, and ½ pea titanium white to create the darkest sky color. Mix ½ pea of the dark sky color with 2 peas titanium white for the medium sky color. Use slightly thinned titanium white to paint the sky closest to the flower and butterfly. Then, paint the medium sky tone on the rest of the background. Stipple between the two colors to blend, and then sweep the brush back and forth slightly to blend further. Add the darkest blue to the outer edge of the sky and the side of the frame, using the same technique to blend the darker and lighter blues. Extend the color up the sides of the leaves, flower, and butterfly.

2 **Paint the leaves.** Mix ½ pea Payne's gray with 8 peas cadmium light yellow. Thin this light green mixture slightly; then, paint the tops of the leaves. Mix 2 peas Payne's gray with a little light green mixture and apply it to the base of the leaves, where the leaf tucks under the flower, another leaf, or any depressions in the leaf. Blend them by stippling. Add unthinned titanium white to the tips of the leaves and any high points (not near any of the dark green paints), blending in the white. The leaves on the left show the placement of the dark green, and the leaf on the lower right shows the white highlight.

PAINTING THE BUTTERFLY

3 **Paint the butterfly wings.** Apply slightly thinned cadmium light yellow to the wing near the body. Mix equal parts of this yellow with burnt sienna, and paint a ring around the yellow portion of the wing. Mix 2 peas burnt sienna with 6 peas alizarin crimson, and paint the outer portion of the wing. Blend the three colors together (as shown in the lower wing) and let the paint dry.

4 **Paint the body.** Mix 6 peas burnt sienna with 1 pea lamp black, and paint the body. Highlight the legs and head with unthinned white. Blend the two paints together by stippling.

PAINTING THE FLOWER

5

Paint the flower petals. Mix cadmium light yellow with a small amount of white, and thin it slightly. Paint the depressed portions of the leaves. Apply unthinned white to the higher areas, and blend the two by stippling. Add a small amount of the yellow to burnt sienna to create a golden tone. Apply this to the shadowed areas and blend. Add unthinned burnt sienna to the bases of the petals for deeper shadows, and blend.

TIP

HIGHLIGHTING AND SHADING

Highlights and shadows add dimension to objects. To add a shadow, use a darker tone on an object where the light would not reach or be as strong (the base of the leaf where it tucks under the flower). Add a light highlight to the object where the light source would first hit the surface—usually the highest point. Look at reference photos or other quality artwork for guidance.

6

Paint the center of the flower. Paint the top half of the raised center with yellow mixed with a little burnt sienna. Paint the bottom half of the center with burnt sienna, and blend. Mix 6 peas burnt umber with 2 peas burnt sienna; paint around the base of the center. Blend in the darker colors. Then add a spot of white to the very top. Blend.

ADDING THE FINAL DETAILS

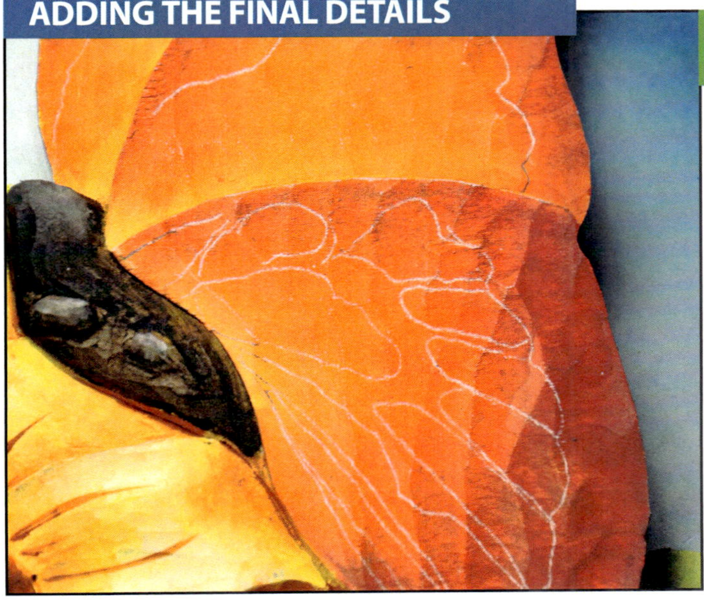

7

Add the petal and wing details. Thin the burnt sienna/burnt umber mixture (from Step 6) and use a script liner brush to paint thin lines radiating out from the petal base. Then, use white dressmaker's carbon to trace the black butterfly markings from the pattern onto the project. Because it is mainly chalk, dressmakers carbon wipes off after the paint is dry. It is available at most fabric stores or can be shop-made (see Tip, at right).

TIP

SHOP-MADE DRESSMAKER'S CARBON

Color a piece of tissue paper with white chalk, turn the paper over, and use it to trace the pattern onto the butterfly.

8 **Paint the black butterfly markings using unthinned lamp black.** Then barely dampen a brush with thinner and tap the edges of the black to make it look a little ragged. Let the paint dry.

materials & **tools**

MATERIALS

- Basswood, 2" (5.1cm) thick: 8¾" x 14" (22.2cm x 35.6cm)
- Artist oils, such as Winsor & Newton: alizarin crimson, burnt sienna, burnt umber, cadmium light yellow, lamp black, Payne's gray, Prussian blue, raw sienna, titanium white
- Odorless thinner
- Wire: 20-gauge, 26-gauge
- Glue: cyanoacrylate (CA)
- Dressmaker's carbon

TOOLS

- Jar for thinner: glass
- Assorted brushes: round, flats synthetic, bristle blenders
- #1 script liner, 2 each
- Needle

The author used these products for the project. Substitute your choice of brands, tools, and materials as desired.

9 **Add the leaf veins.** Mix 8 peas white with ½ pea of the light green used to paint the leaves in Step 2. Thin the mixture slightly; then use the script liner brush to paint the veins. Use a needle to punch holes in the areas for the legs and antennae. Bend 20-gauge black wire to shape for the legs. Then, bend 26-gauge black wire for the antennae. Use cyanoacrylate (CA) glue to affix the wires in the needle holes.

10 **Add the white markings to the butterfly.** Use unthinned white and the script liner brush. Note that the markings are not symmetrical in shape—this adds to the realism. Paint the frame top, outer edge, and back with thinned raw sienna.

Working with Latex Paint

For with a durable finish that is easy to blend, try latex house paint

I am a professional sign carver, and when I'm making a sign that will hang outdoors, I paint it with exterior latex paints. Yes, house paint. They are designed for the outdoors, so they stand up to the weather. Like acrylic paints, latex paints are water-based, so they clean up easily with soap and water, but latex paints have a longer drying time than acrylics, which allows you to blend them more easily. They still dry relatively quickly, though, so you don't have to wait long to recoat. This method will give you solid coverage—you will not see any woodgrain when you use these paints in layers as described.

Getting Started

Use the pattern on page 23 and your choice of tools to carve the piece.

Paint

I use semigloss or satin latex paint; you may use flat (matte) paints if you prefer. Use exterior formulations if you intend to put this carving outside. Most stores will mix small sample-size cans of paint if you ask. I use the brand California Paints, which I've painted with for years with great success.

BASECOATING THE CARVING

1 **Prime the carving.** Apply two coats of primer to the front and back of the carving. Allow each coat to dry before applying the next one.

2 **Basecoat the design.** *Note: Latex dries quickly enough that you should complete each pumpkin or leaf before moving on to the next.* Mix 2 peas yellow with 1 pea red to make a light orange, and paint the bottom half of one pumpkin. Paint the top half yellow, and then stipple along the line where the two colors meet to blend them. Repeat the process for the other pumpkin. Mix 3 peas yellow with ½ pea blue to make a light green; apply this to the leaves.

3 **Paint the sky.** Using dark blue, paint the sky area, continuing the paint up the sides of the leaves and the inside edges of the frame. Immediately add some white to the upper right side of the sky, and blend the edges of the white into the wet sky paint. This will be the glow of the moon that you will paint later.

4 **Paint the pumpkin stems.** Use a warm medium gray, such as barrel stave. Highlight the centers with a little white. Paint the outside and top of the frame with the gray. Allow everything to dry. *Note: The primer shows through the base coat in places, making the leaves appear to be more than one color although you have only applied one coat of paint to them so far.*

DETAILING THE PROJECT

5

Add the leaf details. Mix 1 pea yellow with 3 peas blue to make a dark green. Beginning with the leaf on the far left, paint the top half and edges of each leaf with the light-green mixture used in Step 2, and paint the center with the dark green. Blend the two colors well. Remember, complete each leaf before starting the next.

6

Highlight the leaves. Dip one corner of the blending brush in white. Position the brush so the white will hit the edge of the leaf, and then blend the white into the greens.

7

Highlight the pumpkins. Paint the top half of each pumpkin with yellow. Paint a second coat of light orange just below the yellow, and blend them together. While the paint is still wet, add some white to the top "humps" of the pumpkins and blend it in. Paint the leaf between the pumpkins using the technique explained in Steps 5 and 6.

8

Recoat the sky. Paint the sky dark blue and blend white in the glow area around the moon like you did in Step 3. Paint the moon white, and let the paint dry.

9

Paint the leaves that curl over the base of the carving. Use the techniques explained in Steps 5 and 6 to paint these leaves and to highlight the tips with white.

10 **Paint the leaf curls.** Paint the inner portion of the curl dark green and the outer portion light green. Blend the two colors, add a little white to the edge of the curl, and blend the colors again.

11 **Add leaf veins.** Mix white into the light green to make a celery color. Use a script liner to add veins to the leaves.

12 **Add shadows to the pumpkin bottoms.** Add crimson to the bottom of each pumpkin and to the depressions between the humps. Use a damp—not wet—blending brush to blend the red. Darken the red by adding ½ pea black to 2 peas crimson, and repeat the process a little lower on each pumpkin to add more shadow.

13 **Finish the stems.** Paint the pumpkin stems with the warm medium gray. Add white to the top center of the stem and blend it in.

14 **Finish the moon and sky.** Paint the moon white again, and then blend some warm medium gray into the lower portion and along the side of the frame. Dip the end of a paintbrush into white or very light blue paint and dot the sky with stars in a random pattern. Paint the edges, side, and back of the carving with warm medium gray.

materials & **tools**

MATERIALS

- Pine, 2" (5.1cm) thick: 8¾" x 14" (22.2cm x 35.6cm)
- Primer (use exterior if the sign will be outside): white
- Latex paint (use exterior if the sign will be outside): black, crimson red, dark blue (such as California Navy Teal #DE5832), lemon yellow (such as California Confidant Yellow #DEA117), warm medium gray (such as California Barrel Stave #DE6216), white
- Container (for water)
- Tin foil or other palette
- Paper towel or cloth

The author used these products for the project. Substitute your choice of brands, tools, and materials as desired.

TOOLS

- Assorted brushes: synthetic and bristle
- #1 script liner

Using Thinned Paints
ON AN UNPRIMED SURFACE

For luminous, translucent color, create washes by mixing paint with plain water

You've learned how to create stunning details using unthinned acrylics on a primed base—but thinned paints on a raw wood base create an entirely different look. Adding paint in washes allows you more control over the finished product.

Getting Started

Carve the project using the pattern on page 24 and tools of your choice. Clean the cuts and remove any fuzzies. Sand the sides to a smooth finish.

Assemble your painting materials. Slightly thin all of the color mixes with water, unless otherwise stated, so you can see a little woodgrain through the paint.

PAINTING THE BACKGROUND

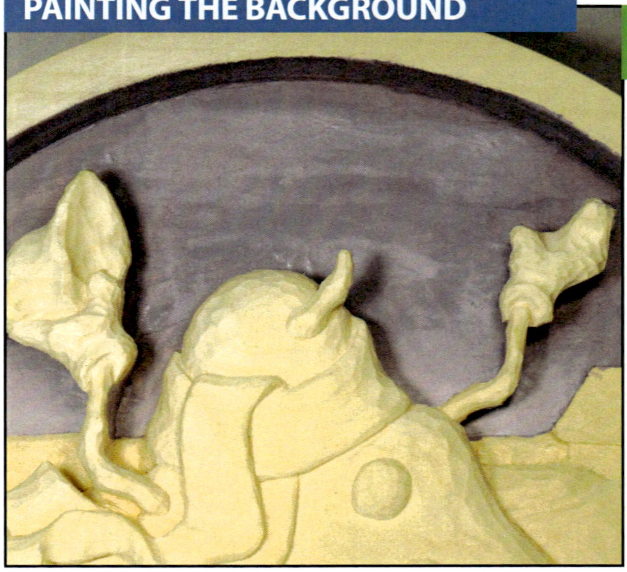

1 **Paint the sky.** Mix 4 peas Payne's gray with 1 pea naphthol crimson to make a deep purplish-blue. Mix 1 pea of this dark purple with 4 peas white to create a lighter tone. Spray the darker color with water so it doesn't dry, and then paint the lighter mixture to the sky below the snowman's arms, beginning in the lower left area under the hat. Paint the horizon white, and blend the colors together. Remember to paint the sides of the frame, the hat, and the stick arm. Paint the rest of the sky using this technique.

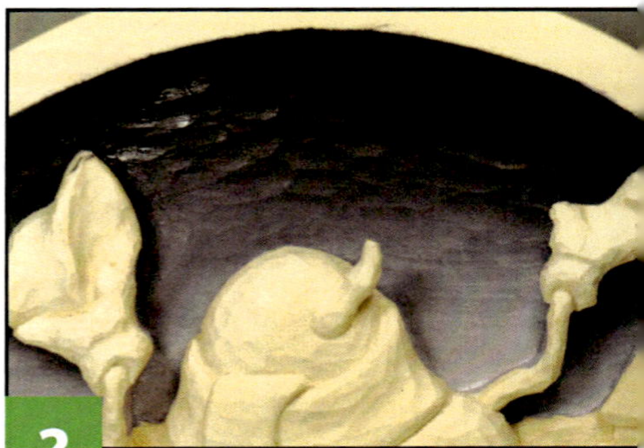

2 **Darken the top of the sky.** Apply the dark purple mixture to the top area of the sky and blend it into the lighter color. If the paint is too dry, dip the brush in water, blot it on a paper towel or rag, and blend. The damp brush will help the paints blend more easily. Spray the dark mixture lightly with water and save it to shade the snow (see Tip at right).

3 **Paint the snow.** Thin white slightly and paint the snowman and snow.

4 **Add the first tree.** Create a dark green by mixing 3 peas Payne's gray with 1 pea yellow. Do not thin this mixture. Use a small pointed brush to tap in an irregular, fuzzy, tall, cone-shaped pine tree. Save this mix for later use.

5 **Detail the tree.** Highlight the right side of the tree with unthinned yellow, and tap it slightly to blend. Repeat Steps 4 and 5 to add a line of trees across the horizon. Vary the heights and shapes of the trees. Add snow to the trees by tapping them with unthinned white in an irregular pattern.

6 **Shade the snow.** Add a little white and a little water to the dark purple. Beginning with the snow in the hill behind the house, paint the top of the hill white, add the purple shade to the sides and bottom, and blend. Continue to paint the snowy landscape in this way, hill by hill.

TIP

SAVING PAINT

To save a paint mixture for later, spray it lightly with water, cover it with a piece of foil, and press the foil firmly to drive out any air.

7 **Add highlights and shadows to the hilltops.** Dip a brush in water, blot it on a cloth, and use it to blend the white into the hilltops. Add darker shadows where needed by adding a little of the dark purple and blending it in the same way.

8 **Paint the path.** Paint the sides of the path with the dark purple and the center of the path white. Blend the two together. Stipple (dot) unthinned white on the sides of the path to resemble snow.

PAINTING THE SNOWMAN

9 **Shade the snowman.** Use the dark purple. Start with the head and work down. Paint the base of the head purple, and paint the rest of the head white. Blend the two with a damp brush. Paint the purple on the bottom and left side of the body, around the buttons, and under the scarf. Paint the rest of the body white and blend with a damp brush. Use a pencil to draw stripes on the scarf, mittens, and hat.

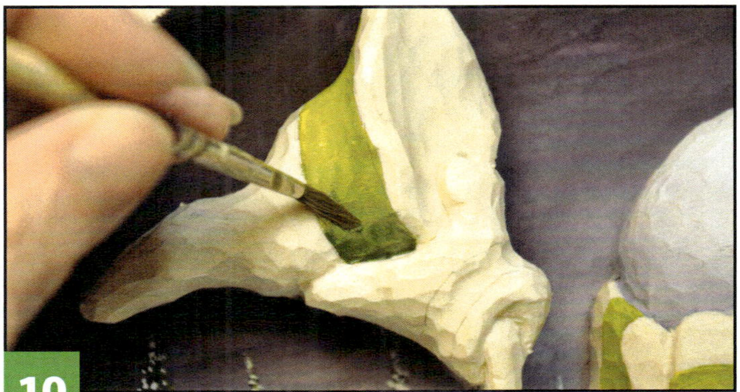

10 **Paint the green stripes.** Add a small amount of the dark green mixture to 1 pea yellow to make a light green. Thin the mixture slightly, and paint the stripes on the scarf, mittens, and hat. Highlight the stripes immediately with yellow, and blend. Apply thinned pine tree mixture to the shadowed areas and blend with a damp brush.

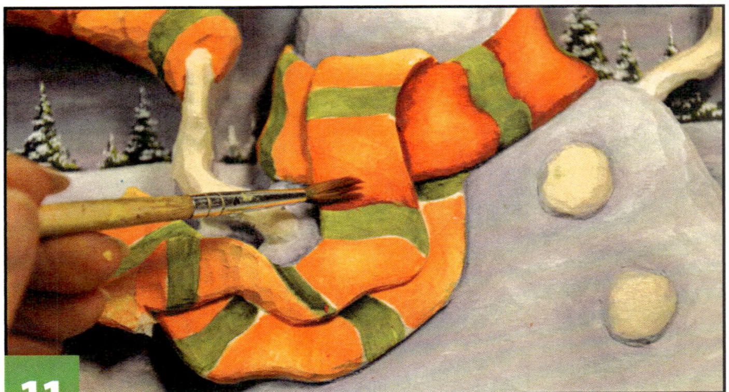

11 **Paint the orange sections.** Mix ½ pea naphthol crimson with 5 peas yellow to make light orange, and thin it slightly. Paint the orange areas on the scarf, hat, mittens, and nose. Highlight these areas with yellow, and blend. Then, add a little white and blend. Mix equal parts naphthol crimson and burnt sienna to shadow the orange. Dampen each section with water and paint the mix along the edges; repeat for the base of the nose. Blend the shadows with a damp brush.

12 **Paint the remaining hat and scarf details.** Add one pea dark red and ½ pea black to the shading color from Step 11. Paint this mixture in the hollow of the hat opening, and blend it in with a damp brush. Repeat the process for the openings of the mittens. Use a script liner brush to paint lines between the stripes on the hat, scarf, and mittens with the slightly thinned dark green mixture.

13 **Paint the rest of the snowman and fence.** Dip the end of the paintbrush in black and dot on the eyes and mouth. Paint the buttons black, and highlight them with white. Mix 1 pea each raw umber and white to make a warm gray, and paint the stick arms. Highlight the arms with unthinned white, and blend with a damp brush. Add shadows with raw umber, and blend. When dry, drybrush the arms with white. Repeat this process for the fence posts.

COMPLETING THE PROJECT

14 **Begin painting the house.** Paint the chimney using the technique for the snowman's arms in Step 13. Paint the front wall of the house with the naphthol crimson/burnt sienna mix. Paint the side with the darker red mix used for the hollow of the hat (naphthol crimson/burnt sienna/black). Paint the trim with raw sienna, and paint the roof white. When dry, paint the door and windows white, and let dry. Scrub some white above the chimney for smoke.

15 **Detail the house.** Mix a little yellow with a little burnt sienna for a golden tone. Thin the mixture and apply a light coat (or glaze) over the windows. Thin raw sienna and glaze the door with it. Add thinned purple to the snow on the roof, and blend it in with a damp brush.

materials & **tools**

MATERIALS

- Basswood blank, 2" (5.1cm) thick: 8¾" x 14" (22.2cm x 35.6cm)
- Pencil
- Tin foil
- Paper towels
- Acrylic paint, professional quality: black, burnt sienna, naphthol crimson, Payne's gray, raw sienna, raw umber, titanium white, yellow light

TOOLS

- Container for water
- Assorted brushes: rounds, flats, blenders
- #1 script liner
- Spray bottle of water

The author used these products for the project. Substitute your choice of brands, tools, and materials as desired.

16 **Paint the frame.** Mix equal parts of raw umber and white. Thin the mixture slightly and paint the frame, sides, and back of the carving.

Welcome Signboard

Pair any of the projects in this booklet with a Welcome sign. Pattern for the sign is on the inside back cover.

Pattern Section

Patterns for all of the projects in this booklet are on the following pages.

Note: When carving, refer to the numbers to determine the carving order (i.e., start with leaf 1, then do leaves 2, 3, and 4).

Tulip Plaque Pattern

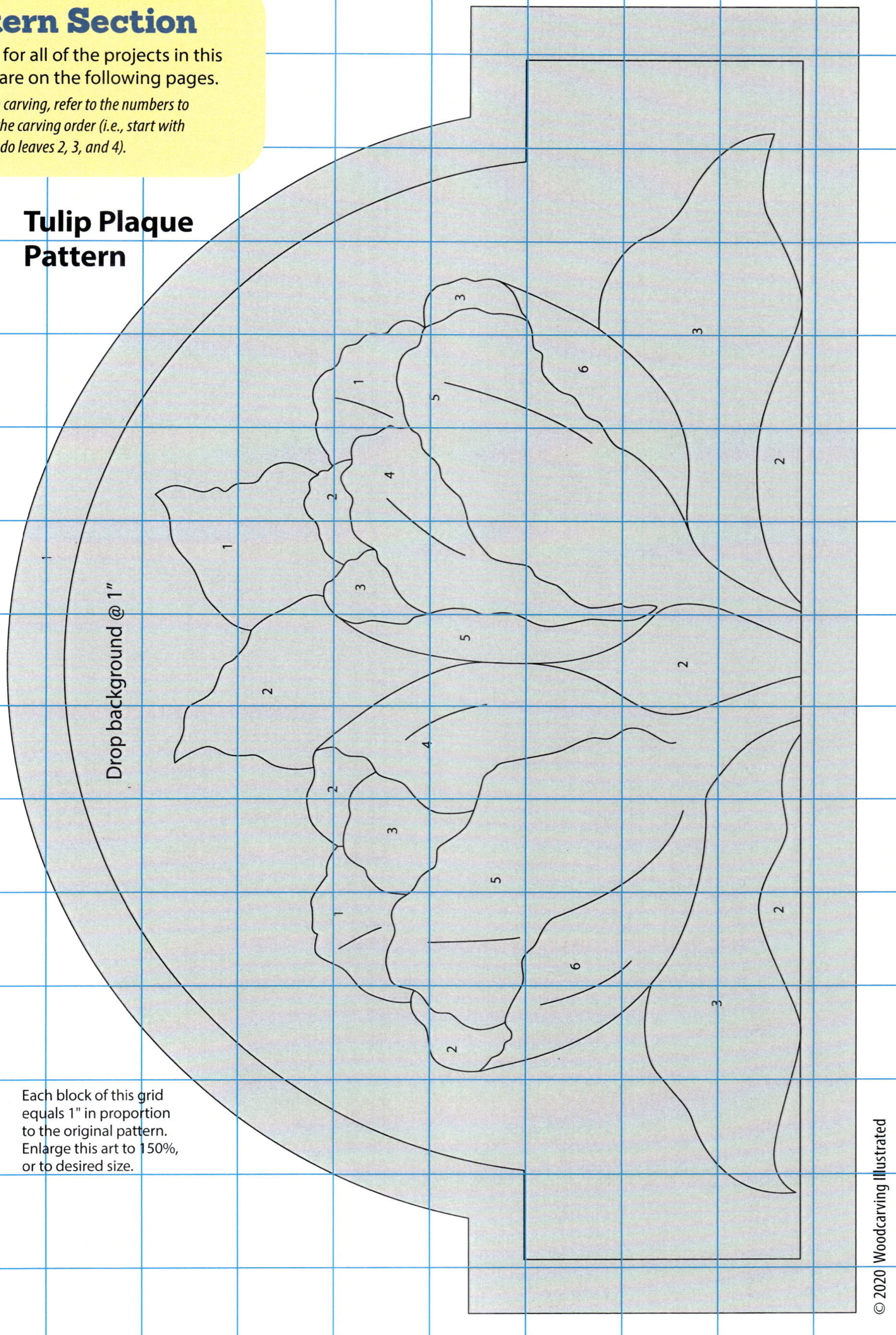

Each block of this grid equals 1" in proportion to the original pattern. Enlarge this art to 150%, or to desired size.

Butterfly Plaque Pattern

Each block of this grid equals 1" in proportion to the original pattern. Enlarge this art to 150%, or to desired size.

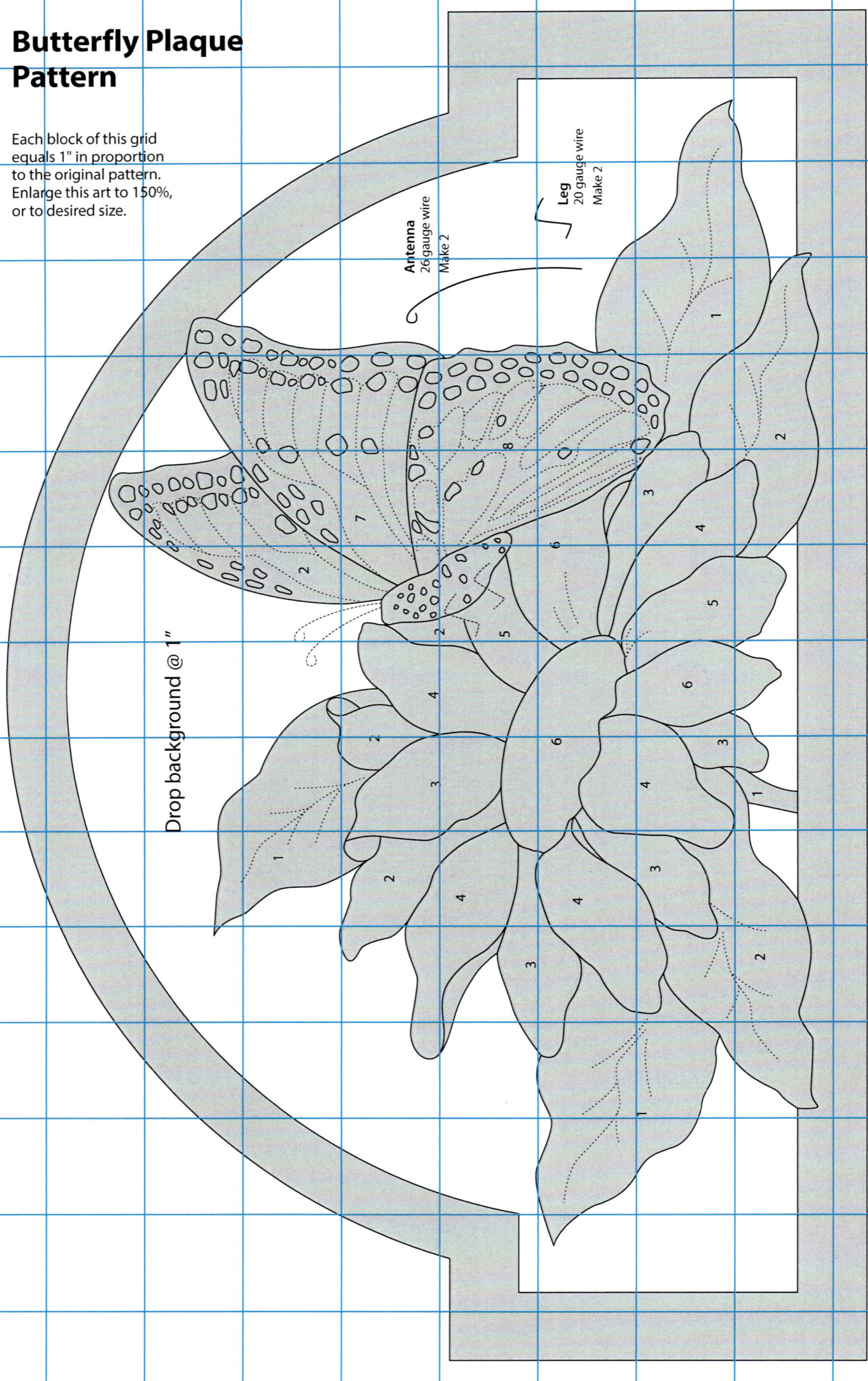

Pumpkin Plaque Pattern

Each block of this grid equals 1" in proportion to the original pattern. Enlarge this art to 150%, or to desired size.

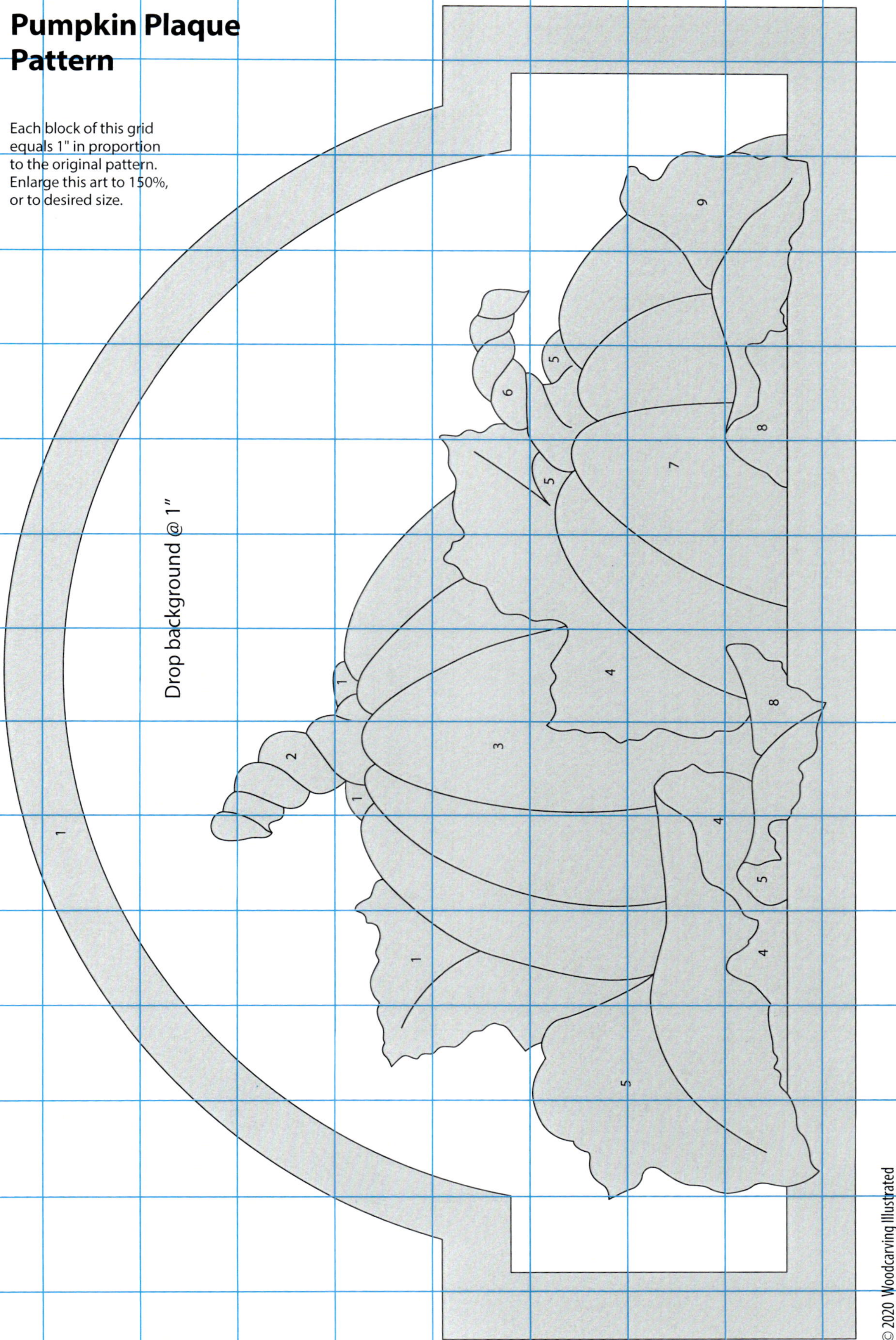

Snowman Plaque Pattern

Each block of this grid equals 1" in proportion to the original pattern. Enlarge this art to 150%, or to desired size.

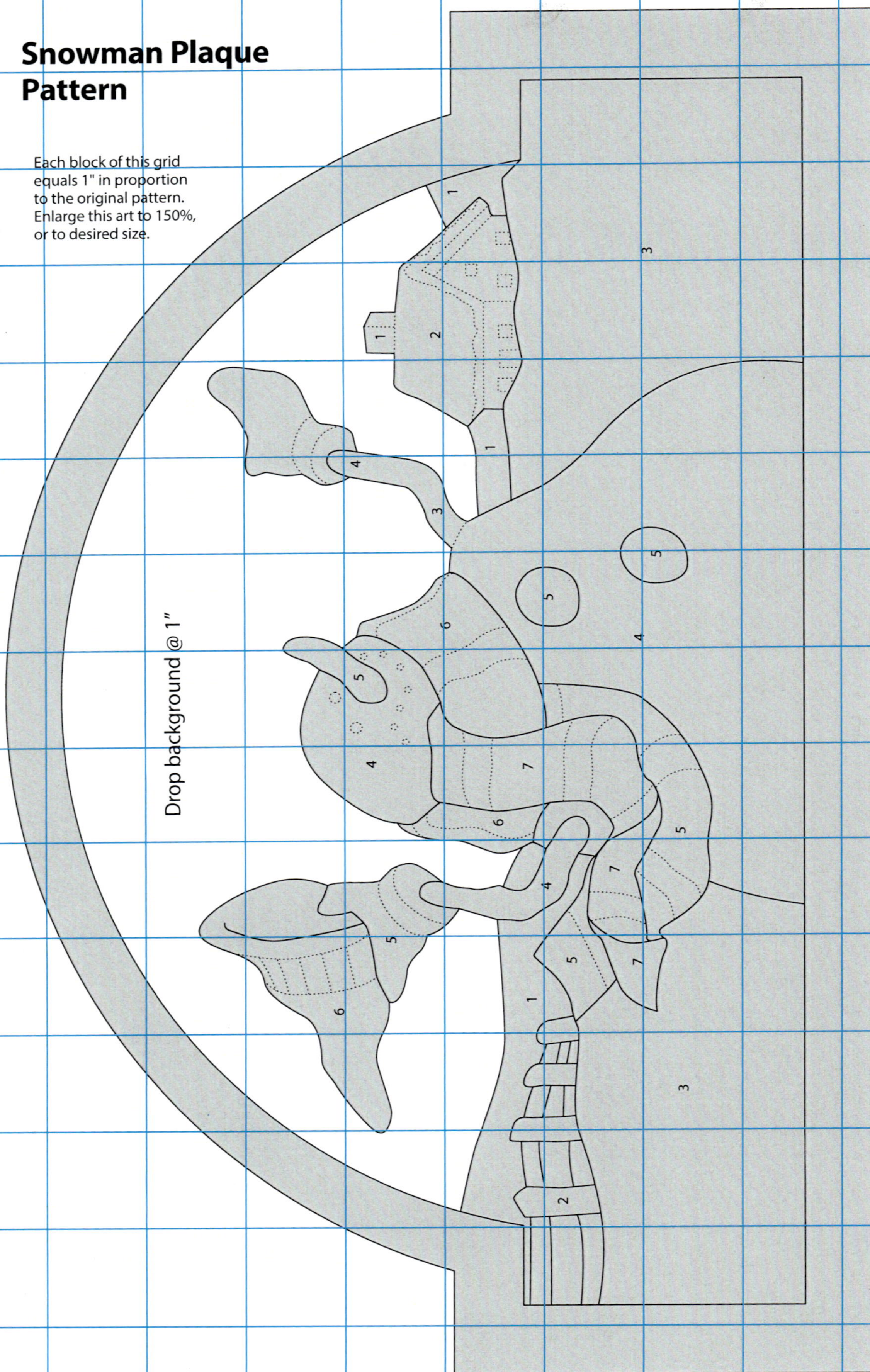